P9-DGE-498

Florence Hershberger

from Marvin and Alice Newcomer

Blessed Are You

Jane Merchant

BLESSED
ARE YOU

ABINGDON PRESS & *New York • Nashville*

BLESSED ARE YOU

Copyright © 1961 by Abingdon Press

All rights in this book are reserved.
No part of the book may be reproduced in any
manner whatsoever without written permission of
the publishers except brief quotations embodied in
critical articles or reviews. For information address
Abingdon Press, Nashville 2, Tennessee.

Library of Congress Catalog Card Number: 61-12767

Scripture quotations unless otherwise noted are from the
Revised Standard Version of the Bible and are copyright
1946 and 1952 by the Division of Christian Education of
the National Council of the Churches of Christ in the
U.S.A.

Poems previously published are copyright 1958, 1959 by the
David C. Cook Publishing Company; 1959, 1960 by The
Curtis Publishing Company; 1959, 1960 by Farm Journal,
Inc.; 1959 by The Graded Press; 1958, 1960 by *Life and
Health;* 1960 by the McCall Corp.; 1956, 1958, 1959, 1960,
1961 by Jane Merchant; 1957, 1958, 1959, 1960 by The
Methodist Publishing House; 1958 by *The Nashville Ten-
nessean* Sunday Magazine; 1959 by Lovick Pierce, Pub-
lisher; 1960 by the Salvation Army, Inc.; 1955, 1958, 1960
by the Sunday School Board of the Southern Baptist Con-
vention; 1960 by *These Times;* 1960 by *Venture;* 1952 by
The Washington Evening Star.

SET UP, PRINTED, AND BOUND BY THE
PARTHENON PRESS, AT NASHVILLE,
TENNESSEE, UNITED STATES OF AMERICA

ACKNOWLEDGMENTS ❧

Many of the poems in this book have appeared previously in magazines and newspapers. Acknowledgment is expressed to the following:

To *Adult Student* for "For Any Year."

To *Bible Lessons for Adults* for "In Swaddling Clothes."

To *The Christian Science Monitor* for "Arrival," "First Things," "For Growing," "Grandmother's Gift," "Munificence," "Renewing Fellowship," "To Welcome Travelers," "Winter-ripened," and "With a New Book."

To *The Church School* for "Good Afternoon," "Having These," "On Gathering Morning Flowers," "To Each," and "Twofold."

To *Classmate* for "Recommendation," "To Be Alive," and "The Saving One."

To *Epworth Notes* for "Ananias Remembers," "Joy in the Morning," and "The Wall with a Window."

To *The Farm Journal* for "For a New Home" and "Theme."

To *The Ladies' Home Journal* for "Country Ways."

To *Life and Health* for "The Hidden Singer," "Sky for Five," and "The Young One."

To *Mature Years* for "For a Busy Friend."

To *McCall's* for "Gift Card."

To *The Nashville Tennessean* Sunday Magazine for "Solitary."

To *The New York Times* for "Candle at Midday."

To *The Saturday Evening Post* for "The Faint Hour," "March Willow," "Retired," and "Time Out."

To *Sunday Digest* for "High Journey" and "To Share."

To *These Times* for "The Answer of the Heavens."

To *Together* for "Cup into Cross," "For the Seeking," "If We Ask," and "Song of Thanks."

To *Upward* for "A Christmas List," "The Lavish Lord," and "The Shining Day."

To *Venture* for "Hospital Aides' Prayer."

To *The War Cry* for "Betrayals" and "The Heedless Women."

To *The Washington Evening Star* for "Biography."

To *Workers with Youth* for "Of Old and New."

PREFACE ❧

The old advice to count our blessings is apt to seem rather irritating when we need it most, but I am confident that it is good advice, because the world's best sermon begins with a list of blessings.

It may seem like a rather unaccountable list of blessings, to be sure, and one that has little to do with us personally. Like James's "Count it all joy, my brethren, when you meet various trials," it assumes a higher mathematics than most of us have learned. We think of a blessing as something that makes life easy for us; and few of us, however sincere may be our response to the beautiful sayings and life of our Lord, find it really easy to cease being self-centered, self-sufficient, and self-assertive. For most of us it requires constant daily effort to become humbly trustful, receptive, and obedient to the spirit of Christ which alone can make us truly hungry for righteousness, merciful, pure, and peaceable.

It is, however, the most rewarding effort any of us can ever make. I pray that these meditations on the Beatitudes may help those who use them draw nearer to the One who lived them perfectly, and to live in his grace, and to receive his assurance, "Blessed are you."

JANE MERCHANT

CONTENTS ☙

VII. BLESSED ARE THE PEACEMAKERS

VIII. BLESSED ARE THOSE WHO ARE PERSECUTED FOR RIGHTEOUSNESS' SAKE

I

BLESSED ARE
THE POOR IN SPIRIT

He . . . taught them, saying: "Blessed are the poor in spirit, for theirs is the kingdom of heaven."　　　　—*Matt. 5:1-3*

THE MOUNT OF THE BEATITUDES

It was a little mountain, with no name
For overwhelming altitudes, no claim
To being earth's most majestic, most sublime;
It was a mountain weary folk could climb.
And on the lowly mountain small winds went
Sighing across the grasses meekly bent
Beneath the weight of many trampling feet,
And sparrows twittered, finding seeds to eat
In merciful supply, beneath the pure
Blue sky, and home trees peacefully secure.
　　And here the searching people heard him speak
His blessing on the humble, mournful, meek,
The needy, merciful, and pure, and all
Peacemakers, and those whom men mistreat, and call
Hard names for living thus. The startling words,
Mingled with chirps of confident small birds,
Brought guilty consternation and disdain
To many, and to others wistful pain,
But many hearers, eagerly receiving,
Found joy beyond belief in sure believing.
　　No inaccessibility excludes
Us from the Mount of the Beatitudes.
If we but firmly, finally put aside
Our anxious selfish righteousness and pride
And strive in earnest love to do his will,
Our hearts may hear him saying, "Blessed," still.

O blessed Lord, grant us grace to believe and to live in the joy of thy blessing. For thy love's sake. Amen.

At that time the disciples came to Jesus, saying, "Who is the greatest in the kingdom of heaven?" And calling to him a child, he put him in the midst of them, and said, "Truly, I say to you, unless you turn and become like children, you will never enter the kingdom of heaven. Whoever humbles himself like this child, he is the greatest in the kingdom of heaven.

Whoever receives one such child in my name receives me."

—*Matt. 18:1-5*

CHILD IN THE MIDST

Forgivingly the Master smiled
At quarreling men. "Unless you turn
Becoming like this little child,
Eagerly, humbly glad to learn
And glad to serve the least and last,
Not seeking power, you cannot be
Within the kingdom. Hold this fast:
Receive a little child, and me."

His arms around the child, he thought,
Perhaps, of tales his mother told
Of great and powerful men who brought
To one poor house, rich gifts of gold;
Who, schooled in all that books reveal,
With wealth and honors given them,
Were humbly, wisely glad to kneel
Before a child in Bethlehem.

Thou knowest, our Father, that like the first disciples we are slow to learn the first discipline of thy kingdom, of turning resolutely away from all our prideful self-assertion. Forgive and help us, Lord. Help us to become as little children in unpretending honesty, in willingness to acknowledge our dependency on thee, in open eagerness to learn and to serve, for his sake who became a child for our sakes. Amen.

For by grace you have been saved through faith; and this is not your own doing, it is the gift of God—not because of works, lest any man should boast. For we are his workmanship, created in Christ Jesus for good works, which God prepared beforehand, that we should walk in them.
—*Eph. 2:8-10*

SYMBOL

The holly bush we planted
Upon a Christmas day
Is shining green in August,
Is glossy green in May,
And always in December
The richly lustrous sheen
Of welcoming wreaths upon our door
Has kept our Christmas green.

"I'm glad we planted Christmas,"
Some of us always say,
While going to the holly bush
For green to give away—
Most fully, thankfully aware
That, though we help it grow,
Our Savior planted Christmas
Within us, long ago.

We thank thee, heavenly Father, for all the good we have, and for all the good we have done and may do, knowing thou art the ultimate source of all. All our abilities are of thy giving, all our accomplishments of thy empowering. Lord, may we ever use thy gifts with humble reverence, knowing that to whom much is given, of him much shall be required. In Christ's name. Amen.

MUNIFICENCE

Now in the golden season
Take to yourself much treasure
Of maple gold, of aspen gold
Presented without measure—

Presented with surpassing
Pure liberality
From all the gleaming branches
On every wealthy tree—

And with no merit demanded
Of you; with no bereaving
Of other wealth. This gold requires
Only your receiving.

Father who givest all, give us receiving hearts. There is so much that could be ours, there is so much that thou wouldest give us, Lord, if only we were willing to receive it. Help us to take time to let the beauty of thy world enter into our hearts and become our own, creating in us thankfulness and joy. Help us to take thought to be eagerly receptive to the truth of thy word, letting it become active and vital in our lives, creating in us righteousness and peace. Help us, O Father, truly to receive the riches thou art ever offering us, and to be gratefully aware of all we owe to thee. In Christ's name. Amen.

Lord, my heart is not haughty, nor mine eyes lofty: neither do I exercise myself in great matters, or in things too high for me.

Surely I have behaved and quieted myself, as a child that is weaned of his mother: my soul is even as a weaned child.

—*Ps. 131:1, 2 (K.J.V.)*

GOOD AFTERNOON

Alone on a hill,
Resting in sun,
Grass-silent, rock-still,
These things I have done:

Outgrown a resentment,
Made peace with a sorrow,
And laid by contentment
For many a morrow.

Being silent and small
And letting light through
I have done all
I most needed to do.

Lord of the hill of blessing, we thank thee for all tranquil listening hours. We thank thee for respite from tense concern with responsibilities that seem too great for us. We thank thee for the peace that comes when we relinquish our own desires, even for things that have seemed most dear and necessary to us, in obedience to thee. Lord, may we learn to empty ourselves, that thou mayest fill us with thy light and thy love, thy peace and thy power. In Christ's name. Amen.

When men are cast down, then thou shalt say, There is lifting up; and he shall save the humble person.

—*Job* 22:29 (K.J.V.)

FOR GROWING

Today I close my door
And hope no one will come
Because I am too small
For anyone to see.

Sometimes flowers clench their petals,
Snails curve within sealed pearl,
Moles nudge deep into darkness.
I close my door.

Hiding precedes revealing
And smallness is for growing.
Tomorrow I will open
Many doors.

Help us to know, O God of returning and rest, when it is time for us to stop our busy efforts even to help others and to wait in lowliness and smallness for thy help. Grant us to seek in quiet days, O Father, so vital an experience of strengthening prayer that when there is no quiet or privacy we still may shut the door of our spirits against all distractions and pray to thee in secret, and be instantly uplifted and renewed. In Christ's name. Amen.

Pride goes before destruction,
and a haughty spirit before a fall.
—*Prov. 16:18*

BIOGRAPHY

She said, the day that dealt her
The devastating blow,
"Now though my heart is shattered
No one shall ever know.
No one shall offer pity
And smile with secret spite
For I shall go in calm by day
And quietness by night."

She lived, austerely lovely,
With grave, patrician grace
Of cool, corrected manner
And pale, perfected face.
She armed her heart with hauteur
And hid her hurt in pride
And no one knew; and no one
Wept for her when she died.

Keep us, O God, from the distrustful pride that shuts our hearts away from human fellowship and sympathy, that refuses to acknowledge any need, and that turns away from any offered help. Keep us most of all from the pride that shuts us away from fellowship with thee, that refuses to acknowledge our need for thy salvation in Christ, and that turns away from thy persuading love. Grant us to know our constant need of thee, and to seek for and receive thy constant help. Through Christ our Lord. Amen.

In a severe test of affliction, their abundance of joy and their extreme poverty have overflowed in a wealth of liberality on their part. —II Cor. 8:2

GRANDMOTHER'S GIFT

Because Grandmother sewed to earn
Her children's bread through arduous years
The little coat she made for me
Showed artistry with cloth and shears.

Because she had a knowing heart
The sturdy coat had double seams—
And hidden pockets where a child
Could safely store her merriest dreams.

Because she kept her spirit bright
While toiling for her daily bread
The cherished coat that warmed me well
Was joyous, flaming red.

We remember with gratitude, dear Lord, all that we owe to others. We thank thee for all who have loved us with a valiant love, who have given our childish hearts gifts greater than we could know or understand. For all their unnoticed sacrifices for our sakes, for all their tears unshed lest we be saddened, for all their cares concealed lest we be anxious, we pray thy richest blessings, thy deepest consolations to them, Lord, now and forever. In Christ's name. Amen.

As sorrowful, yet always rejoicing; as poor, yet making many rich; as having nothing, and yet possessing everything.

—II Cor. 6:10

THE APRIL SISTERS

How many times, and in how many Aprils,
Have these two sisters hung out new-washed clothes
To dry in petaled air! Clothes boiled outside
In an iron kettle on their flowering ridge
In the far days when they were young together
And rich in laughter, rich in dogwood bloom,
And cardinal song, and warm love for each other,
Though rich in little else. And through life's changes
They visited over the mountain when they could,
Hanging their children's clothes in April sun,
Sharing the years of seldom quite enough
Of anything but sky, and love, and laughter;
And sharing the loss of loved ones, sharing the loss
Of each one's best beloved, and helping each other
To live with the long loneliness of waiting.
And now in the latest April they are together
Again, for a little while, in a little house.
Stiffly and haltingly they hang the clothes,
And, talking of grandchildren, plucking a sweet
   shrub bloom,
They linger in the white light of dogwood blossoms
And hear a cardinal sing, and laugh together.

We thank thee, heavenly Father, for all who live rich lives undaunted by the lack of many temporal goods. Help us to learn from such lives, Lord, firm dedication to high personal ethics, steadfast refusal of all unworthy means of gain, and the joyous peace of being content with such things as we have. Amen.

23

A man lame from birth was being carried, whom they laid daily at that gate of the temple which is called Beautiful to ask alms of those who entered the temple. Seeing Peter and John about to go into the temple, he asked for alms. And Peter directed his gaze at him, with John, and said, "Look at us." And he fixed his attention upon them, expecting to receive something from them. But Peter said, "I have no silver and gold, but I give you what I have; in the name of Jesus Christ of Nazareth, walk." —*Acts 3:2-6*

IT WAS NOT GOLD

> Their very look roused my anticipation;
> They had an air, somehow, of men with much
> To give; I gazed with eager expectation
> Of gold or silver; then I felt a touch
> Lifting me from the pallet I had lain
> On all my weary life—I caught my breath,
> Fearing to fall, and heard words, clear and plain,
> "Walk, in the name of Christ of Nazareth!"
>
> And so I walk, and do my daily task
> And earn my bread, who begged for all my years.
> This Christ does more than we can think or ask—
> He gives us life, in spite of all our fears!
> All praise to him in whom I have believed,
> It was not gold or silver I received.

Forgive us, Lord of abundant life, our anxious seeking for assurance of material security and comfort when thou art seeking to give us power to live adventurous, constructive lives of vital usefulness. Give us, Lord, and help us to guide others to the gift of joyfully victorious life in Christ. In his name. Amen.

You know the grace of our Lord Jesus Christ, that though he was rich, yet for your sake he became poor, so that by his poverty you might become rich.　　　　　*—II Cor. 8:9*

THE LAVISH LORD

How prodigal the Savior is,
Sowing the poorest land
With rich abundances of seed
With an unsparing hand.

How prodigal the Savior is—
And yet he cannot spare
A single lamb from all the flock,
A bird from all the air.

And never can the lavish Lord
Of galaxies above
Afford that one bewildered soul
Be stranger to his love.

O Christ our Lord, we thank thee for the overwhelming love that brought thee to this world of fumbling people, and that sustained thee through the daily denials of thy earthly ministry. We thank thee for the love poured out in terrible humility upon the cross that thou mightest reach and save the worst and best, the mightiest and least, all equally in need, all equally desired and dear to thee. May we who know thy love, O Christ, be filled with thy deep yearning that all for whom thou lived and died may know and live. Amen.

Since then we have a great high priest who has passed through the heavens, Jesus, the Son of God, let us hold fast our confession. For we have not a high priest who is unable to sympathize with our weaknesses, but one who in every respect has been tempted as we are, yet without sinning. Let us then with confidence draw near to the throne of grace, that we may receive mercy and find grace to help in time of need.
—*Heb. 4:14-16*

DEPENDENCE

Thou knowest, Lord of all, how much I need
Thy wisdom, having little of my own.
Without thy guidance nothing can succeed.
Without thee I am utterly alone.

Without thy constant help I cannot bear
The ever-increasing sorrow of the days,
Nor conquer small temptations to despair
That trip my heart in unexpected ways.

Without thy love I have no love to give,
Without thy spirit I am nothingness.
O fill me with thy life, that I may live;
Give me thy blessing, Lord, that I may bless.

Thou who dost understand, and sympathize, and love, thou who dost care supremely for each separate needy soul, we bring our needs in confidence to thee. We bless thee, O Lord of blessing, for clarity in our confusion, for strength in our weakness, for rest in our weariness, for thy fulfilling of our emptiness. Amen.

II

BLESSED ARE
THOSE WHO MOURN

II

BLESSED ARE
THOSE WHO MOURN

Blessed are those who mourn, for they shall be comforted.
—*Matt. 5:4*

PLAIN COMFORT

Whenever any loved familiar friend
Or neighbor learns the lonely ways of grief,
My mother bakes large loaves of bread to send,
Knowing no surer way to give relief.
"There is a time for cookies, pies, and cakes,"
She says. "A time for fancy, rich desserts,
But not when trouble's in the house; it takes
A sturdier food to ease the sudden hurts
That come to all. Bread has the quiet power
Of sun and earth to reassure folks' hearts
And give them courage in the saddest hour.
In easier times they relish cakes and tarts,
But when a trouble's new they need, instead,
The good, plain comfort of a loaf of bread."

God of compassion, who alone canst heal the brokenhearted and save the crushed in spirit, most fervently we pray that all who mourn may know thy saving help in all its fullness. Help us with sensitive and tender hearts to share their sorrow and to do the little things that may assure them of our deep concern and ease the painful stress of troubled days. In Christ's name. Amen.

But we would not have you ignorant, brethren, concerning those who are asleep, that you may not grieve as others do who have no hope. For since we believe that Jesus died and rose again, even so, through Jesus, God will bring with him those who have fallen asleep. —*I Thess. 4:13-14*

FOR ONE BEREFT

I have no right to say that it is wrong
That you, who lost the ones you loved with all
The strength and fervor of your heart, should long
To keep their memory vivid, should recall
Each word, each look, lest any fade, and tend
The thought of every dear and lovely thing
They ever did, with anxious care, and spend
Your days in passionate remembering.

I have no right, no right at all, to say
That it is wrong; but I have known the pure
Sharp desolation of each lonely day
And all the aching darkness you endure,
And I am sure, as I am sure of light,
It would be wrong to say that it is right.

Give courage to the hurt ones, Lord, according to thy promise, that they may not withdraw from life and spend their days in grieving memories. Help them most gratefully to trust their loved ones to thy love, now and forever, assured that with thee all is well with them. And help them in this confidence to seek out others here who need the understanding sympathy that only grief can teach, who need the thought and care they lavished on their lost ones, and to give it unreservedly, with love. Through Christ our Lord. Amen.

Blessed be the God and Father of our Lord Jesus Christ, the Father of mercies and God of all comfort, who comforts us in all our affliction, so that we may be able to comfort those who are in any affliction, with the comfort with which we ourselves are comforted by God. —II Cor. 1:3

THE SAVING ONE

> One there was who smiled at me
> After my bereaving.
> Others came with pitying looks
> To assist my grieving.
>
> Numb my heart, and dull my mind,
> And strange all faces were,
> But one there was who smiled at me,
> And so I smiled at her.

We thank thee, Lord of blessing, for all those whose steadfast faith has strengthened us in time of deepest need. Help us, our Father, though knowing well the strange bewilderment and the long heartache that follow any loss, to share with those who mourn the firm assurance that with thee no loss is overwhelming and no grief unbearable. In the name of Christ. Amen.

Rejoice with those who rejoice, weep with those who weep.
—*Rom. 12:15*

MULTIPLE

One letter brought good tidings,
Another, news of sadness;
So my heart is feeling
Mingled grief and gladness.

So my heart, the whole day,
Is busy interweaving
Thanks for one who's happy
With prayers for one who's grieving.

Seldom does a day come
Single in emotion
To one engaged in living
Life with full devotion.

Father in heaven, we thank thee for the privilege of participating in the joys and sorrows of our friends. We thank thee that everyone who cares deeply for others always has reason for joy as well as for sorrow. And we thank thee most of all, O loving and merciful Father, when those whose mourning we have shared are comforted and given the garment of praise for the spirit of heaviness. We praise thee in the name of Christ. Amen.

Father of the fatherless and protector of widows
   is God in his holy habitation.
God gives the desolate a home to dwell in.
                                    —Ps. 68:5-6

GRANDMOTHER'S GARDEN

The winter after he died
She ordered far more
Brilliant seed catalogs
Than ever before.

She had no garden then;
The farm had gone
When he did. The catalogs
Were for hoping on.

Turning the pages of pictures
Of huge, indomitable flowers
She could believe in spring
Through dark, frozen hours.

Their children would find a way,
Understanding her basic need
For putting down roots again.
They were grown of good seed.

She had a house and garden
The summer after he died,
And a bundle of seed catalogs
Verified.

God of steadfastness and encouragement, may the hearts of
all lonely and desolate people be filled with peaceful trust in
thee, and may their brave faith be abundantly fulfilled. Amen.

> Do not cast me off in the time of old age;
>   forsake me not when my strength is spent.
>   —*Ps. 71:9*

RETIRED

> Streets creak with cold, and deepening snow
> Conceals what earth there was to see,
> But now there is no need to go
> And bring in extra wood, as he
> Half started to. You merely turn
> Electric heat up higher, here.
> You don't go plunging through the stern,
> Hard-crusted, steely atmosphere
> To break ice in the horses' trough
> And milk each blandly trustful cow,
> And shoo excited chickens off
> Until you've shelled their corn. Not now.
> Nothing waits, here in town, for you.
> You take your ease. That's all you do.

Remember in thy abundant faithfulness, O Father, all those who are no longer able to work at their accustomed tasks, and grant that they may find other needed and deeply satisfying work to do. Give to all thy people through all their days, O Lord, the assurance of being deeply loved and needed; keep them from the paralyzing sense of uselessness and maintain them always in dignity and honor. In Christ's name we pray. Amen.

Now may our Lord Jesus Christ himself, and God our Father, who loved us and gave us eternal comfort and good hope through grace, comfort your hearts and establish them in every good work and word. —II Thess. 2:16-17

THE APRIL SHADOW

Always in April, on her quiet face
Where calm acceptance of denial rested
At other times, we saw the shadow's trace—
The shadow of old patience newly tested.
We saw how wistfully her eyes would follow
Explorers of faint winding pathways, bound
Into the secret depths of glen and hollow
Where April's earliest blossomings were found.

They brought her wildwood flowers, shy and fair,
And she would smile, like one who almost sees
Their forest home, and almost breathes the air
Where shadows of new leaves on April trees
She never walked beneath, dance lightly on
The April earth she never walked upon.

Thou who dost know the yearning in the hearts of the handicapped and the ill, and whose ears are ever open to their cry, uphold their spirits always by thy grace. Strengthen their steadfast courage, Lord, and reward abundantly their patient determination to build good, helpful lives in spite of circumstances. And grant to them all, O God of comfort, a constant overcoming in every daily trial. In Christ's name. Amen.

Comfort ye, comfort ye my people, saith your God.

—*Isa. 40:1 (K.J.V.)*

HOSPITAL AIDES' PRAYER

For all the sweet ones, Father,
So patient and so still,
So pleased if someone smiles at them,
So worn with being ill,
So grateful for a book to read,
Or the least of summer's flowers—
O be with them, abide with them,
Through all the tedious hours.

And for the cross ones, Father,
Who grumble and complain
In furious resentment
Of helplessness and pain,
Who are not pleased or grateful
For anything we do—
O be with them, abide with them
The aching, long hours through.

And give us patience, Father,
And help us truly care
For all the lonely people
Who have too much to bear,
And let us not forget them,
We who are whole and free.
O be with us, abide with us
In serving them and thee.

We thank thee, heavenly Father, for the privilege of bringing any help to others in their need. In Christ's name. Amen.

But he, desiring to justify himself, said to Jesus, "And who is my neighbor?"
—*Luke 10:29*

WHO IS MY NEIGHBOR?

He is my neighbor, well I know,
The child with eager puzzled face
Who wonders why he may not go
With paler children to their own place
To learn with them of what is true
And what is just and fair and right—
Is truth divided? May one do
All good things better if one is white?

He is my neighbor, and I weep
In sorrow and remorse for him;
And yet, the stubborn men who keep
Him separate, who strive to dim
His eager eyes, impelled by greed
And prejudice and guilty fears—
They are my neighbors, and they need
No less than he, my prayers and tears.

Oh, may I never turn away
From either oppressors or oppressed,
But ever faithfully work and pray
That all may be redeemed and blessed,
Opposing with relentless love
The wrongs men do themselves and others
Till by the grace of God above
We live in harmony as brothers.

Grant us grace, O God, to mourn with active godly sorrow till the evils that men do are done away. In Christ's name. Amen.

Whatever was written in former days was written for our instruction, that by steadfastness and by the encouragement of the scriptures we might have hope.   —*Rom. 15:4*

TO SHARE

> Not for my comfort only,
> Not for my aid alone,
> The star-gleam in the darkness,
> The sparkle in the stone.
>
> Not for my single solace
> Is ponderous silence stirred
> By inward songs, by gentle
> Small easings of the Word.
>
> The dark, the stone, the silence
> Are not mine to explain
> But bear; and mine to share the star,
> The sparkle, the refrain.

Our heavenly Father, we thank thee for all the good words and comfortable words which have spoken to our most personal needs from the pages of thy Book. We have not words enough to thank thee fully, Father, for the words that bring us comfort in our sorrow, encouragement in our weariness, guidance in our perplexity, rebuke and warning in our waywardness, and always the assurance of thy everlasting love. Grant, O God, that we may so love and live the words of life that our lives may speak thy word to other hearts. In the name of our Lord. Amen.

Truly, truly, I say to you, you will weep and lament, but the world will rejoice; you will be sorrowful, but your sorrow will turn into joy. —*John 16:20*

THE HEEDLESS WOMEN

It would have been more prudent to remain
Quietly at home, not risking Roman ire.
Perhaps the dawn air held a hint of rain;
They might have found some comfort near a fire.

It would have been more practical to send
The cost of spices to the crowding poor
As a memorial tribute to their Friend,
And safer; they need not have left their door.

They hurried through the early morning gloom
Heedless of their own comfort and protection;
And found the empty testifying tomb
And heard the tidings of the resurrection.

O saving Lord, impress upon our hearts that it is not in seeking our own comfort that we are comforted, but in our acts of self-forgetting love. And give us grace that in our most distressful times we may find ways to render helpful service to thee and to thy people. Turn thou our thoughts, O Lord, from mournful dwelling on our sorrows and ourselves, and grant that all our sorrows may be turned to joy in thee. Amen.

For our light affliction, which is but for a moment, worketh for us a far more exceeding and eternal weight of glory; while we look not at the things which are seen, but at the things which are not seen: for the things which are seen are temporal; but the things which are not seen are eternal.

—II Cor. 4:17-18 (K.J.V.)

CUP INTO CROSS

When dogwood blooms are still
Small untouched cups
They are all bruise-brown,
Not white.

But the bruises grow into crosses
Wholly white, save at the very edge,
And all the lowly trees gleam in white glory
Of wounds outgrown.

God of Gethsemane and Calvary, help us bravely and willingly to drink whatever cup of suffering may be within thy will for us. Help us unflinchingly, unfailingly, to deny ourselves, and take up our little crosses day by day, and follow him who gave his life for us. In his name we pray. Amen.

III

BLESSED ARE
THE MEEK

Blessed are the meek, for they shall inherit the earth.

—*Matt. 5:5*

TO WELCOME TRAVELERS

The grass could not be greener than it is
If men should ride a rocket to the moon,
Nor could the sky appear more purely blue
Even when viewed from Venus at high noon,
And all these pansies that enrich the grasses
With multiplicities of difference
In similarity, are marvelous
As any blossoms gathered on immense
Fields of Polaris. However many go
On interstellar journeys to prove their worth,
Many will stay behind to welcome them
To pansies and the faithful green of earth.

We bless thee, O Lord God, creator and sustainer of the green familiar earth and all the farthest reaches of the enormous universe. We praise thee that though men take the wings of the morning and dwell in the uttermost parts of the sea or of the sky, even there thy hand shall lead and thy right hand uphold them, and that none can ever adventure beyond the presence of thy Spirit. As men have gained knowledge and power by humbly studying and meekly co-operating with thy physical laws, so may thy people, Lord, through devoted obedience to thy moral and spiritual laws win lasting victories for righteousness and justice on this earth. In the name of Christ. Amen.

And Mary said, Behold the handmaid of the Lord; be it unto me according to thy word. —*Luke 1:38 (K.J.V.)*

And he was withdrawn from them about a stone's cast, and kneeled down, and prayed, saying, Father, if thou be willing, remove this cup from me; nevertheless not my will, but thine, be done. —*Luke 22:41 (K.J.V.)*

IN THE BEGINNING WAS THE WORD

Before the star was seen,
Before the song was heard,
"Lord, be it unto me
According to thy word."

Before the lilies flowered
In early morning sun
Beside an empty tomb,
"Thy will, not mine, be done."

Before our hearts can share
The Christmas joy, or see
The Easter radiance,
"Lord, as thou will with me."

Our Father, we thank thee for thy amazing meekness, which will not force thy heavenly will on us, but ever leaves us free and waits for our consent. May we be humbly aware, Lord, of the responsibility of freedom, and of the loss to us and to others if we do not respond to thee. Thou who dost always give to those who ask with earnest sincerity the power to will and to do thy good pleasure, grant us so to ask and to receive that thy purposes of blessing may be fully accomplished in our lives. In Christ's name. Amen.

The poor man died and was carried by the angels to Abraham's bosom. The rich man also died . . . ; and in Hades . . . he lifted up his eyes, and saw Abraham far off and Lazarus in his bosom. And he called out, "Father Abraham, have mercy upon me, and send Lazarus to dip the end of his finger in water and cool my tongue; for I am in anguish in this flame." But Abraham said, . . . "Between us and you a great chasm has been fixed."

—*Luke* 16:22-24, 25, 26

THE CHASM

If it had been permitted
Would Lazarus have gone
With water for the thirst of one
Who let him hunger on
Through all his aching lifetime
And never thought to share
More than a meager, careless crumb
Of all his sumptuous fare?

"Send Lazarus!" The rich man
Was most presumptuous still.
One who had begged beside his gate
Must surely do his will.
And had no yawning chasm
Forestalled the benison
How eagerly, how quickly,
Would Lazarus have gone.

Keep us aware, O Lord, how impassable the chasm can become between those who care for earth's needy ones and those who care only for themselves. Keep us aware that by our daily choices we are constantly becoming more careless or more caring, more selfless or more selfish, more greedy or more generous; and grant that all our choices may be thine. In Christ's name. Amen.

By your words you will be justified, and by your words you will be condemned. —*Matt. 12:37*

SOLITARY

The left-alone lady
Lives in a house
Visited mostly
By mailman and mouse.

The left-alone lady,
The old ones say,
Was young and pretty
And witty and gay—

Oh, always witty!
Her friends were the best,
But she mentioned each one
With a well-turned jest.

And so she became
In a while and a while
The left-alone lady
Who doesn't smile.

Forgive us, Lord, for all our thoughtless speaking. Forgive us for all our self-important attempts to be considered clever and entertaining, without considering how our words may wound. Grant us to be so yielded and controlled by thy spirit that even in our most relaxed, informal conversations we speak only courteous and kindly words. Keep us from criticizing and condemning others, and give us courage to protest with pleasant firmness when unkind and harmful words are uttered in our presence. In Christ's name. Amen.

Beware of practicing your piety before men in order to be seen by them; for then you will have no reward from your Father who is in heaven. —*Matt. 6:1*

THE HIDDEN SINGER

Once, in the dark, a bird
Sang to my heart, and stirred
More joy than heart could claim.
It did not tell its name,
Nor had I time to linger
To seek the hidden singer.

The birds I know have sung
Gay songs, forever young,
But never the counterpart
Of the song within my heart.
The purest notes belong
To the anonymous song.

O God, who knowest all the things we are loath to admit to ourselves, thou knowest the persistent desire of our hearts for appreciation of the good we do. Thou knowest, Lord, our petulance when others seem ungrateful and our inward dismay when our best efforts pass unnoticed. Help us, Lord, to learn from the birds who sing for joy of singing, not for praise; and grant us to find such creative joy in the work we do that we may be truly unconcerned about receiving credit for it. In Christ's name. Amen.

Blessed is the man that walketh not in the counsel of the ungodly, nor standeth in the way of sinners, nor sitteth in the seat of the scornful. But his delight is in the law of the Lord; and in his law doth he meditate day and night. And he shall be like a tree planted by the rivers of water, that bringeth forth his fruit in his season; his leaf also shall not wither; and whatsoever he doeth shall prosper.   —*Ps. 1:1-3 (K.J.V.)*

THEME

Over and over, I have tried to say—
Or, this being much more suitable, to sing—
What trees have meant to me. The tremulous sway
Of their adventurous fragile leaves in spring
On blossom-scented cool air, sanctified
By homeward wings and luminous sunset glow
Has given me gentle glories that abide
Within my heart henceforward; and I owe
Much I have learned of grace and fortitude
To bare trees beautiful through winter's stress,
And always their great tallness has renewed
And verified my faith in upwardness.
So all my songs say only that every tree
That I have known lives evermore in me.

For thy law written in the grace and strength and usefulness of trees we thank thee, Lord. May our lives be rooted and grounded in thy love, and may we ever send roots downward and bear fruit upward, for thy glory. In Christ's name. Amen.

The Lord will open to you his good treasury the heavens, to give the rain of your land in its season and to bless all the work of your hands. —*Deut. 28:12*

ARRIVAL

Not yet—not quite,
Though the hasty wind is spinning
Leaves from the trees, it is only the flurried light
That resembles the slant of rain.

Not quite—not yet,
Though the air is silver and flowing
Not a single circle of wetness
Has flowered on the dusty street.

But now—but now
One drop has fallen—another,
And the street is a running mirror
Of shattered blossoms of rain.

Lord, when some needed blessing seems delayed, and our spirits are dry and sick with hope deferred, grant us the blessing of patient trust in thee. However stunted with lack our souls may feel, let us never forget that the dry season can be the season of greatest growing, if we endure it with abiding faith. Save us, O Father, from the shame of having doubted and complained, when thy renewing comes, as come it will. In Christ's name. Amen.

Blessed by the Lord be his land,
with the choicest gifts of heaven above,
and of the deep that couches beneath,
with the choicest fruits of the sun,
and the rich yield of the months,
with the finest produce of the ancient mountains,
and the abundance of the everlasting hills.
—*Deut. 33:13-15*

OCEAN VISIT

The ocean is all around us on these mountains.
The waters go up to the mountains from the seas
On hurrying wings of clouds; and mighty fountains
Of the deep are broken up on giant trees
That pattern ancient earth's exalted acres
With their innumerable arrays of green.
Beneath the thunderous pounding of huge breakers
These inland peaks are luminously marine.

We mountain people have no need of going
To distant shores to know the ocean well,
For all the rich exuberance of growing
And light and shade that hold us in their spell,
Perpetually renewed and various,
Are ours because the ocean visits us.

We thank thee, our Father, Lord of heaven and earth, that thy blessings come to us wherever we are—on shining mountain peak or in shadowed valley, on blazing desert or ocean-freshened shore. We thank thee that there is no place so lonely, obscure, and forgotten by men that thy grace and thy peace cannot reach whoever calls upon thee. For all thy blessings poured out on us and others we praise and bless thy holy name. Amen.

Blessed be the Lord, who daily loadeth us with benefits, even the God of our salvation.   —Ps. 68:19 (K.J.V.)

THE SHINING DAY

> All day the sky's deep blue has shone
> With vivid gentleness. All day
> A little sunlit wind has blown
> Rose-fragrances our way.
>
> There has been no intemperate glare
> Nor any overwhelming heat,
> Only the deep sky, coolly fair,
> And the small wind, coolly sweet.
>
> There is no more than this to tell
> Now that the shining day is done;
> Save that our hearts have loved it well
> From sun to sun.

Creator of all, we thank thee for the shining beauty of ordinary days. We thank thee that when our hearts are at peace with thee and all our ways fully committed to thy keeping, we are able to receive and enjoy our heritage of earth's abundant beauty. Thou knowest how often our eyes are dulled with self-concern and our spirits clouded with presumptuous worry, so that no loveliness of earth or sky is truly ours. Lord, help us so to trust thee and to praise thee that we may truly inherit this shining earth. In Christ's name. Amen.

Fear not, for I am with you,
    be not dismayed, for I am your God;
I will strengthen you, I will help you,
    I will uphold you with my victorious right hand.

                                   —*Isa. 41:10*

TWOFOLD

Holding on and letting go
Are the arts the soul must know;

Holding on to God in stress,
Letting go all bitterness;

Holding on with faith entire,
Letting go your own desire—

Concentrate your soul upon
Letting go and holding on.

He who holds will let you go
Only if you will it so,

And, when all your strength is gone,
All his love is holding on.

We thank thee, heavenly Father, for thy everlasting strength, for thy upholding power. We thank thee, O victorious Lord, that when we yield ourselves and all our heart's desires to thee in confident trust, we may receive continuous victory over all the inward foes that ever assail us. Through Christ our Lord. Amen.

IV

BLESSED ARE
THOSE WHO HUNGER
AND THIRST FOR RIGHTEOUSNESS

Blessed are those who hunger and thirst for righteousness, for they shall be satisfied. —*Matt.* 5:6

FOR THE SEEKING

"Oh, Master, send these crowds away.
They hunger now, at end of day."

"They need not go away," he said.
"You give them meat. You give them bread."

"We give? To this great crowd you see?
This scanty fare?" "Bring it to me."

They brought. He blessed, and said, "Now give,
That all the seeking ones may live."

With the little that they could provide
The multitude was satisfied.

"Send them away," I sometimes plead
When people crowd me with their need.

"They hunger, Lord—and so do I.
How can I help, or even try?"

"Bring me the little you possess
And give the needy what I bless,"

He says, as he will always say,
"They need not go away."

We thank thee, Lord, for thy eternal "Come." We thank thee that in all thy days on earth thou didst not send the crowds away till they were satisfied. We know, and yet forget, O Lord, that in our weariness, discouragement, and need there is no overcoming save by coming unto thee. We come to thee now, Lord, and wait thy blessing. Amen.

And he fasted forty days and forty nights, and afterward he was hungry. And the tempter came and said to him, "If you are the Son of God, command these stones to become loaves of bread."

—*Matt. 4:2-3*

Jesus said to them, "I am the bread of life; he who comes to me shall not hunger, and he who believes in me shall never thirst."

—*John 6:35*

TO ALL WHO HUNGER

Alone in arid wilderness,
Tormented by long strain and stress,

In desperate longing to be fed
He left the stone unturned to bread.

To all who hunger, lost, alone,
He will not offer any stone,

("He fed himself, he was divine,
He never met a need like mine.")

But the assurance, full and free,
That he was tempted even as we,

And, having suffered every need
That any of us know, can feed

Us in all earth's bewildering strife
With the unfailing bread of life.

Thou who didst hunger that we might be fed with living bread, thou who didst suffer thirst that we might drink of living water, we thank thee that there is no need of ours unknown to thee, nor any pain of ours thou dost not share. We thank thee that thou knowest our temptations, Lord, and that thou art patient with us when we fail. Help us to deny all wrong desires. Amen.

Or what man of you, if his son asks him for a loaf, will give him a stone? Or if he asks for a fish, will give him a serpent? If you then, who are evil, know how to give good gifts to your children, how much more will your Father who is in heaven give good things to those who ask him?　　　—*Matt. 7:9-11*

SOME BETTER THING

Lord, I would be obedient to thy will,
Not longing for what is not given me,
Assured some better thing awaits—and still,
The tears flow, Father, till I cannot see.
Forgive me, Lord, forgive me that I yearn
For anything thy pure love can deny.
Armor my heart against the swift return
Of the insinuating, stealthy "Why?"

Grant me to triumph, Father, over days
And weeks when all my world seems wholly wrong.
Grant me abiding patience and deep praise,
Grant me to turn my longing into song;
So shall I be more strengthened and consoled
Than by the blessing, Lord, thou dost withhold.

Father in heaven, all our desires are before thee, and our groanings are not hidden from thee. And we believe that thou who spared not thy own Son for our salvation wilt give us with him all things that are for our good. And we praise thee, our Father, in his name. Amen.

And when you pray, you must not be like the hypocrites; for they love to stand and pray in the synagogues and at the street corners, that they may be seen by men.   —*Matt. 6:5*

IF WE ASK

Lord, if we ask for courage
Let us always be
Ready to accept
Each adversity
And peril and adventure,
Because through these alone
Can courage ever truly
Be strong and fully grown.

Lord, if we ask for patience
Let us always take
Quietly each blunder
And every mistake
And all the small shortcomings
Of others and of ours,
Since from irritations
Genuine patience flowers.

Lord, if we ask the taking
Of our trials away
Teach us that such words as these
Are what we really say:
"We have no desire
For growing, after all.
Make us selfish cowards,
Lord, keep us weak and small."

Grant us, Father, complete sincerity in all our praying and in all our living. In Christ's name. Amen.

Brethren, do not be children in your thinking; be babes in evil, but in thinking be mature. —I Cor. 14:20

FIRST THINGS

> Never return
> To the towering hill,
> The enormous river,
> The mighty mill.
>
> Whoever returns
> Is apt to see
> A dwindled homestead,
> An outgrown tree.
>
> But the love first given you,
> The love first known,
> Is always larger—
> If you have grown.

God of all growing, help us, as we grow older, to grow in appreciation of all that has been done for us and given to us by others. As we usually find that the places of our childhood are smaller than we remembered them, may we realize that the people of our childhood were larger in spirit than we could understand. We thank thee for the sacrifices, the devotion, and the patience of parents, ministers, teachers, and friends—for all whose lives left on our lives a deep impress for good. Through the kind things they did to make us happy we learned to trust in life, and love, and thee. Lord, may thy grace reward them evermore. In Christ's name. Amen.

For I tell you, unless your righteousness exceeds that of the scribes and Pharisees, you will never enter the kingdom of heaven. —*Matt. 5:20*

THE TEACHER

Authentic character, the honest, rare
Original personality and mind
She cherished in her students; one quick flare
Of individuality, not blind
Humdrum conformity to thoughtless ways
In any boy or girl, could bring a keen
Triumphant joy to her devoted days
And give her weary nights a golden sheen.

"Find what is real for you," she urged, "and live
Your own life, not another's; you are too
Important for the truths that you can give
To be lost in what others say and do."

Their love for her who helped their lives expand
Had nothing in it false or secondhand.

We thank thee, Lord, for all teachers who seek with earnest love to encourage in their students deep personal commitment to the highest and the best. Give to all teachers, Father, ability to help the eager, uncertain youngsters in their care to sense the worth and wonder of their lives, and to feel zestful responsibility for fully developing and using all their powers for good. In the name of the greatest Teacher. Amen.

Seek first his kingdom and his righteousness, and all these things shall be yours as well. —*Matt. 6:33*

A CHRISTMAS LIST

You ask my wants for Christmas—oh, I want
So very much; the onward-going trust
That no withdrawal of the light could daunt
Of wise men journeying through desert dust
Believing in a star; and all the strong
Abiding peace of shepherds doing well
Their ordinary tasks, to whom belong
The joyous truths the singing angels tell.

And oh, I long for Mary's quiet grace
Of keeping all the sacred things within
Her heart, and pondering them, lest time efface
The wonder and the awe with careless din.
So very much I want that, surely, he
To whom I give my heart, will give to me.

Lord, in our hearts we know that our deepest needs are not for outward possessions, but for inward peace; not for material abundance, but for moral adequacy. Help us to take time to sort out our fleeting wishes for temporary pleasures from our basic yearnings for eternal joys. Help us to offer earnest prayers for real, specific needs and to wait with gladly expectant hearts for thy response to our requests. In our Savior's name. Amen.

He who supplies seed to the sower and bread for food will supply and multiply your resources and increase the harvest of your righteousness.   —II Cor. 9:10

FOR ANY YEAR

As in all other years, there were mistakes,
Kind acts undone and needful words unsaid,
Quick hurts renewing all the heart's old aches;
And constant earth, and courtesy of bread.

There were, as always, little victories won,
And joyous meetings with new friends and old,
Small, uneventful hours of gentle sun,
And rest beneath the stars' abiding gold.

And now there is the deep impulse renewing
The heart's resolve, beyond mistakes and tears,
For deeper understanding, worthier doing,
As in all other years.

We thank thee, heavenly Father, for thy reviving power, enabling us to put aside the memory of past mistakes and failures and to press on hopefully toward better things. Enable us to be daily transformed by the renewing of our minds, so that we may prove thy good, acceptable, and perfect will in every least endeavor. In Christ's name. Amen.

And he said to them, "Therefore every scribe who has been trained for the kingdom of heaven is like a householder who brings out of his treasure what is new and what is old."

—*Matt. 13:52*

OF OLD AND NEW

Out of the old year I shall keep
Tested friendships, strong and deep,
Certain truths that I have learned,
Sympathy and patience earned
From darkness, and a firmer-souled
Faith in the Lord of new and old.

Into the new year I shall take
Zest for new friends I may make,
Eagerness for learning more
Of truth and patience than before,
And more faith in the Father, who
Is the Lord of old and new.

Father, in whom we live and move and have our being, we thank thee for thy present help in all the days of all our years. We thank thee that our poorest years contained much treasure in the dependable helpfulness of friends, the ever-changing, never-failing beauty of earth and sky, and thy eternal love and grace that are forever new. Lord, as these have not failed us, may we not fail to find new ways of service, new appreciation of our blessings, new, always deepening confidence in thee. In Christ's name. Amen.

What is man, that thou art mindful of him? and the son of man, that thou visitest him?   —Ps. 8:4 (K.J.V.)

But as many as received him, to them gave he power to become the sons of God, even to them that believe on his name.
                                                        —John 1:12 (K.J.V.)

THE ANSWER OF THE HEAVENS

When the young shepherd watched his flocks by night
On the green-pastured hills of Bethlehem
He pondered the heavens with their hosts of light,
Humbly, exultingly considering them,
So infinite in their glory far above him
With no star ever lost, or hurt, or dim—
"Lord, what is man, that thou art mindful of him?
And the son of man, that thou dost visit him?"

To other shepherds on the ancient hills
The answer to the shepherd's question came
In glorious songs of One who bears the ills
Of all his flock, and calls his own by name,
By whose redeeming staff and chastening rod
The sons of man become the sons of God.

Lord, keep our hearts in holy awe before the wonder of the Christmas miracle. Thy answer to our lonely questionings and yearnings is so well known, so necessary, and so dear that we can scarcely imagine life without it. Because thou art the Lord who cares, we feel it had to be; but wert thou not the Lord who cares it never could have been. We thank thee, Lord, that thou art mindful of us even to visiting us to share all of our human sufferings and struggles, even to dying for us on the cross. Help us to use the power thou hast given us. Amen.

V

BLESSED ARE
THE MERCIFUL

Blessed are the merciful, for they shall obtain mercy.

—Matt. 5:7

NOT FOR HIMSELF

His life was mercy,
And though in death
He found no mercy
His final breath
Sought blessing for
Each jeering foe:
"Father, forgive;
They do not know."

Not for himself
Did he obtain
Mercy; for those
Who cause us pain
By words that sting,
Acts that appall—
He wins our mercy
For them all.

O Christ, who never seekest great things for thyself but for us and from us, we thank thee for the infinite mercy revealed in thy living and dying. We thank thee that by thy mercy to us we are enabled to be merciful to others. We thank thee, Lord, that even we, who are most jealous of our rights and most resentful of our wrongs, when we are moved by thy forgiveness, can forgive. Amen.

But do thou for me, O God the Lord, for thy name's sake: because thy mercy is good, deliver thou me. For I am poor and needy, and my heart is wounded within me.

—*Ps. 109:21-22 (K.J.V.)*

TIME OUT

I have given myself a little while
In which to remember how to smile.

I will not think, or speak, or act,
Or weep. I will wait. And the numbing fact

Will grow familiar, and I will face
It—sooner or later—with smiling grace.

I will not wonder, since hearts grow tough,
Whether a lifetime is long enough.

Lord, when our hearts are stunned by unexpected wrong, do for us what we cannot do for ourselves. Help us to know that we have only to be still, and turn to thee, if only by a single upward glance, to be delivered from the temptation to despair of good and to return evil for evil. For thou, Lord, who dost ever return good for evil and blessing for cursing, canst make our hearts tough to endure and tender to forgive. Amen.

For if you forgive men their trespasses, your heavenly Father also will forgive you; but if you do not forgive men their trespasses, neither will your Father forgive your trespasses.

—Matt. 6:14-15

TO BE ALIVE

Not to withhold the heart
From the unexpected dart,
The edged word, keen, unsparing;
Not to withdraw into
The peace that once one knew,
The numb peace of uncaring;

And never to erect
One barrier to protect
From any recurrent thrusting,
But hourly to remain
Accessible to pain,
Forgiving, loving, trusting.

Whatever it is that has hurt us, help us, our Father, to forgive as we would be forgiven, not grudgingly, not contemptuously, not conditionally, but wholly, freely, fully, finally. Fill thou our hearts with understanding sympathy, that our forgiveness may not humiliate but help the one forgiven. Keep us aware, Lord, of how much thou hast forgiven us and how constantly we are in need of thy forgiveness, that we may pray fervently for thy pardon for ourselves and for those who injure us. In Christ's name. Amen.

Again he entered the synagogue, and a man was there who had a withered hand. And they watched him, to see whether he would heal him on the sabbath, so that they might accuse him. And he said to the man who had the withered hand, "Come here." And he said to them, "Is it lawful on the sabbath to do good or to do harm, to save life or to kill?" But they were silent. And he looked around at them with anger, grieved at their hardness of heart, and said to the man, "Stretch out your hand." He stretched it out, and his hand was restored. The Pharisees went out, and immediately held counsel with the Herodians against him, how to destroy him.   —*Mark 3:1-6*

HANDS

A man was there who had a withered hand,
And many men with able hands were there;
Hands stretched out to the needy, to demand
The tithe on herbs, and clasped in obvious prayer,
And always kept fanatically clean,
And quick to wave all common folk away,
And raised in shocked protest when One was seen
To aid another on the sabbath day.

Poor futile, shackled hands, withheld from good
By the hard rigor of a human law!
The withered hand stretched out to One who stood
Angered by self-imprisoned men he saw—
One with a hand that healed, and blessed, and gave,
And was not shortened, that it could not save.

Christ of the wounded hands, may we never withhold our hands from doing good for fear of being misunderstood or hurt. Amen.

But if the wicked will turn from all his sins that he hath committed, and keep all my statutes, and do that which is lawful and right, he shall surely live, he shall not die. All his transgressions that he hath committed, they shall not be mentioned unto him: in his righteousness that he hath done he shall live. Have I any pleasure at all that the wicked should die? saith the Lord God: and not that he should return from his ways, and live?
                                              —Ezek. 18:21-23 (K.J.V.)

THE OPEN DOOR

"They opened the prison door," he said.
"They opened the door and I went out free—
Or so I thought. But the prison door
Is the only one that has opened to me.

"I knew I would have to prove myself,
And I knew I would find the going hard.
I mean to do it. But how do you live
When the doors to employment are locked and barred?

"How do you earn your family's bread
And try to make up for the wrong you've done
When none of the people you've known for years
Will open his door to you—not one?

"I pray to the Lord I may live once more
As an honest man among honest men.
It cannot be that the prison door
Is all that will open to me again."

O saving Lord, save us from distrust of those who have genuinely repented of wrongdoing and trusted in thy mercy. Grant us to trust in the sincerity of their good intentions and to trust them with opportunities to prove their good intentions real. In Christ's name. Amen.

Ye are the light of the world. A city that is set on an hill cannot be hid. Neither do men light a candle, and put it under a bushel, but on a candlestick; and it giveth light unto all that are in the house. Let your light so shine before men, that they may see your good works, and glorify your Father which is in heaven.   —Matt. 5:14-16 (K.J.V.)

CANDLE AT MIDDAY

Now the days lose their sheen.
The sun is negligent and does not kindle
A spark from matted clouds, nor any shimmer
In snarls of rain,
And faded hours fray into ragged night.

An open fire is needed now
With gold and crimson flames exultantly
Multiplied in surfaces of wood,
And glass, and polished silver. Flame should dance
Repeatedly on all unshining days.

Having no open fire, I light a candle
And place it where its light shines on old walnut
And in clear glass, and out into the street,
Making a rippling brightness on its dark.
The days have lost their sheen, but here are shinings.

Our Father, when there is no sunlight to be seen, but only the long dullness of cold rain, help us to keep our candles faithfully burning for thy glory, not our own. In Christ's name. Amen.

But if any one has the world's goods and sees his brother in need, yet closes his heart against him, how does God's love abide in him?
                                                                    —I John 3:17

ON GATHERING MORNING FLOWERS

Lord of the many blossomings of May,
Of pansies, lilies, peonies, and roses,
Giver of every fragrant petaled day,
I thank thee for the grace each dawn discloses.
I thank thee for the gentleness of light
Discovering anew each variation
Of color in the gardens of the night;
I thank thee for recurrent revelation.

Dear Lord of all the shining scented air,
Now while I gather harmonies of blooms
Fill thou my heart with love, that I may bear
To weary people in unchanging rooms
Where light is faint and faith is almost gone
The delicate sure flowerings of dawn.

God of the never-withholding heart, keep us responsive to others' needs and eager to share whatever good we have. Grant us to give material things unstintedly in times of dramatic disaster, to relieve the victims of earthquakes, floods, and fires. And grant us to give tirelessly to the unexciting needs of weary people who require, day after day, the reassurance of loving words and genuine concern. In Christ's name. Amen.

But you, beloved, build yourselves up on your most holy faith; pray in the Holy Spirit; keep yourselves in the love of God; wait for the mercy of our Lord Jesus Christ unto eternal life.
—*Jude 1:20-21*

THE WALL WITH A WINDOW

In a certain stony wall
That shuts the spacious world from view
Chance—or miracle—has made
A space for looking through;

A little blessed window space
Through which imprisoned eyes may see
An upward-going leafy road,
A tiny flowering tree;

And, growing close and pressing inward
Through the window in the wall,
Sprays of blossoms shaped to music,
White and sweet and small.

In whatever walls surround us,
Stubborn walls of grief or pain,
Barred by gates that will not open
While our lives remain,

God's love is a window, showing
Us a wide and leafy land,
And his mercy bell-like blossoms
Sweetly close at hand.

Father in heaven, we thank thee that in the walls of time thou hast made windows that open on eternity. In Christ's name. Amen.

Indeed he was ill, near to death. But God had mercy on him, and not only on him but on me also, lest I should have sorrow upon sorrow.
                                                            —*Phil.* 2:27

JOY IN THE MORNING

> For other mercies, Lord,
> My heart could find the word
> And music of glad praise;
> For orderly calm days;
> Evenings that, hour by hour,
> Brought little stars to flower
> In clusters of delight
> Over the breadths of night;
> And for much good between
> Each dawn, heard, felt, and seen,
> Multiform, many-hued,
> I could voice my gratitude.
>
> But for the life of her
> Without whom dawn would blur
> And all star-blossoms be
> Faded and lost to me—
> Lord, for this utmost gift
> I have no word to lift.
> I watch the dawn skies glow
> And know that thou dost know.

We thank thee, Father of mercies, that when our hearts are too full for any word thou dost accept our silent gratitude, our speechless worship. We know we are not worthy of the least of all thy mercies; yet thou givest us the greatest we can ask. Father, we thank thee. Amen.

I appeal to you therefore, brethren, by the mercies of God, to present your bodies as a living sacrifice, holy and acceptable to God, which is your spiritual worship.   —*Rom. 12:1*

SONG OF THANKS

There should be new ways of saying,
"Thank you, Lord," for a wisp of moon
In a wild rose sky of evening,
For a clover-scented noon,
For a mist of rain on roses,
For a star when night is long,
And for moonlight set to music
In a mockingbird's best song.

There are no new ways of saying,
"Thank you, Lord," for loveliness,
Only the old ways of being
Kind to other hearts' distress,
Only the old ways of loving
Till a heart has been restored,
The old faithful ways of living
Day by day, our "Thank you, Lord."

Lord, as thou hast done for us far more than we could think or ask, help us to do for thee more than we now believe that we can do. Help us to forego the pastimes that tire us to no purpose; help us to keep our minds alert and our spirits sensitive to the things we ought to do. And may we never consider unreasonable any request for our service merely because we would prefer some other work. In Christ's name. Amen.

VI
BLESSED ARE
THE PURE IN HEART

Blessed are the pure in heart, for they shall see God.

—*Matt.* 5:8

THE YOUNG ONE

Seventy years or more ago
She whispered, reverently excited,
Seeing the stars begin to glow,
"Mother, look at the lamps God lighted!"

Seventy years ago or more
She startled the family by joyfully crying
(Not having seen butterflies before),
"Mother, Mother, the flowers are flying!"

And now with seventy years gone by
She is still enchanted with lovely hours,
Seeing the Lord in the starlit sky,
Seeing the flying flowers.

O Christ, who alone art utterly pure in heart, we thank thee that thou hast seen and hast shown us the Father. Help us, Lord, to cleanse our hearts from self-love and self-deception, so that we may daily see thee more clearly and love thee more sincerely. Help us to perceive, as thou dost ever perceive, great possibilities of good in what seem to us humdrum people and hopeless circumstances. And may our vision be ever quick, through all our days, to see thee in the beauty of earth and sky and of lives lived in awareness of thee. Amen.

For as the earth brings forth its shoots,
  and as a garden causes what is sown in it to spring up,
so the Lord God will cause righteousness and praise
  to spring forth before all the nations.

—*Isa. 61:11*

COUNTRY WAYS

"Here we turn the children out
To daisies every summer"—
Grandma's glad to talk about
Our ways to every comer.

"Sturdy, trusty, full of zest,
And lovely altogether,
Daisies make the merry best
Of any soil and weather.

"All that any country needs
Is what the country raises
Where the daisies grow like weeds
And children grow like daisies."

We thank thee, heavenly Father, for all the joyously healthful influences that help to keep our minds and spirits sound and pure. We thank thee for the cleanliness of sunlight, fresh winds, and gentle rains, and for all the color and grace of growing things. We pray for these blessings, Father, for all children everywhere, and for thy help to guard all children from evil, that they may grow happily into ways of sturdy integrity and righteousness. In Christ's name. Amen.

Whoever seeks to gain his life will lose it, but whoever loses his life will preserve it.

—*Luke* 17:33

SKY FOR FIVE

> She has scant time to read, the letter said.
> She has four children under six years old,
> And there is room for little in her head
> Save nursery tales a hundred times retold—
> Or so it seems sometimes. She finds it hard
> To have all other interests pushed aside.
> "But the five of us have picnics in the yard,"
> The letter ended. "And the sky is wide."
>
> Because she knows the sky is wide, I know
> She will find ways to keep her mind aware
> Of thoughts beyond the children, till they grow
> To competence, with their own thoughts to share,
> When she will have new vision to explore
> A sky immensely wider than before.

Creator of all life, grant thy sustaining presence day by day, and hour by hour, to all who are given the care of little children. Ease for them, Lord, the tiredness and the strain, and enable them to be always adequate to their responsibilities and opportunities. Fill their hearts with thy creative love, patience, and wisdom, that they may teach children to love thee and one another joyously, and to live and work together in trustful harmony. In Christ's name. Amen.

The eye is the lamp of the body. So, if your eye is sound, your whole body will be full of light; but if your eye is not sound, your whole body will be full of darkness. If then the light in you is darkness, how great is the darkness!

—*Matt.* 6:22-23

MARCH WILLOW

"That willow leafs too early every year,
And every year its leaves are killed by cold.
You're like it, child, impetuously sincere,
Believing every pleasant thing you're told,
And you'll be chilled by many a snub and slight
As sure as all those green leaves die tonight."

The young girl listened to the gnarled advice
And thought how beautiful the doomed leaves were,
And after stormy days of snow and ice
She saw the willow's bright releafings stir
As greenly on the languid sunlit breeze
As those of any wise untrusting trees.

Father in heaven, grant each of us the single eye that looks for the good and not for the evil in others. Grant us sincere hearts to believe in others' sincerity, hearts that would rather be hurt by trusting too much than risk hurting others by trusting too little. And even when we are hurt by others' inconsistencies and failings, help us, Father, still to perceive and love what is truly worthy in them. In Christ's name. Amen.

But blessed are your eyes, for they see, and your ears, for they hear.
—Matt. 13:16

WINTER-RIPENED

You came to us in our brown chilly season
When this huge earth is winter-shabby,
You with remembered green
Of many English Aprils in your heart.

And we who have not seen
But have ancestral memories of the green
Of England, and the little flowering lanes,
And small sequestered gardens rich with bloom,
Showed you the hills we love, the fields we cherish,
      saying,
"If you could see them when clouds of dogwood
      blossoms float
Over them, and the rose-purple froth of redbud, and
      all greens—"
And then we paused,
Seeing your deep sincerity respond
To the unpretense of bare trees and dark hills
And to the truth of our desire for your delight,
And feeling affection flowering in the warmth
Of mutual understanding, and gladly knowing
This winter-ripened friendship long will be
As green as April in Kent and Tennessee.

We thank thee, Lord, for all whose hearts are honest and sincere, uncluttered by affectation and pretense, and for the reliable friendship of such hearts. In Christ's name. Amen.

A gift is as a precious stone in the eyes of him that hath it.
—*Prov.* 17:8 (*K.J.V.*)

WITH A NEW BOOK

I bought the book for you, but I confess
Quite unabashedly, I read it through
Before I gave it, savoring loveliness
With double relish since it is for you,
Thinking how you will cherish airy phrases
As delicately luminous as snow
That falls through sunlight—and each word that razes
Old forts of lies with one hard clanging blow.

You will not chide because I do not send
This book to you unopened and untried,
A stranger other people recommend;
You will be glad that I have verified
Its worth, and gained the deep abiding pleasure
Of being sure my gift is one to treasure.

We thank thee, Lord, for the warm glow of happiness we feel at finding exactly the right gift for a particular friend. We thank thee for the delight of sharing with those who are sure to appreciate them wise and vital thoughts expressed in vivid words. And we thank thee especially, Lord, when we are privileged to help another person to deeper insight, understanding, and response to the richly beautiful words contained within thy Book of life. We thank thee in Christ's name. Amen.

It is more blessed to give than to receive.   —*Acts* 20:35

GIFT CARD

Whatever gift I give to you is yours.
Give it away, or keep it, as you will.
The special books, the china miniatures,
The little birds carved with beguiling skill—
I shall not peer about your house to see
If they are dusted well and duly shown
To visitors, as treasured things may be.
I made a gift of them, and not a loan.

I know that even gifts sincerely loved
Both for themselves and for the giver's sake
Have in life's many changes often proved
A burden; be relieved of the mistake
Of thinking you must keep a gift I give
(Except my love) as long as you shall live.

Heavenly Father, may all our giving be without inward reservations or withholdings. Grant us to give freely, naturally, and joyously, as we have received thy bounteous gifts, given without measure and without price. In the name of Christ, thy greatest gift. Amen.

And the child grew and became strong, filled with wisdom; and the favor of God was upon him.   —*Luke 2:40*

IN SWADDLING CLOTHES

The little one, the precious one,
The tiny helpless king—
To him we offer praise again,
Of him our carols sing.

We cherish him, the tiny one,
With gentle hearts and merry—
He speaks no daunting words about
A cross for us to carry.

He makes no challenging demands
Nor mentions sins that mar
Our lives; he coos in innocence
And smiles upon a star.

Oh, none today cry, "Kill the babe!"—
We tenderly endeavor
To keep him wrapped in swaddling clothes,
A helpless babe forever.

Help us, heavenly Father, to purify our hearts of sentimentality and selfishness; help us to see not only the appealing babe but the demanding Lord. Grant us to offer him not seasonal emotion but eternal devotion. Help us to meet his high demands for purity, self-denial, and warm concern for the less fortunate, day by day. In his name. Amen.

For God speaks in one way,
and in two, though man does not perceive it.
—*Job 33:14*

Judge not, that you be not judged. For with the judgment you pronounce you will be judged, and the measure you give will be the measure you get. Why do you see the speck that is in your brother's eye, but do not notice the log that is in your own eye?
—*Matt. 7:1-3*

TO EACH

God speaks to each the language he can hear,
In sermons, or in silence of a star,
In tenement and temple, slum and cell,
The voice of God calls to us where we are.

Let each of us give reverent care to heed
The voice that speaks to us, from church or clod,
And let us be, oh, very slow to say
Of the voice another hears, "It is not God."

Father in heaven, help us with undivided hearts and minds to hear and heed thy word for our lives, and to work out our own salvation with fear and trembling. Help us to accept with humility and awe the responsibility thou hast given us as free individuals, and to respect the freedom and responsibility thou hast given others. May our hearts be pure of all temptation to criticize and condemn the efforts of others to follow their understanding of the truth in Christ; keep us from assuming that ways that are not our ways are of necessity not thy ways. In Christ's name. Amen.

Stand up and bless the Lord your God from everlasting to everlasting. Blessed be thy glorious name which is exalted above all blessing and praise. . . . Thou art the Lord, thou alone; thou hast made heaven, the heaven of heavens, with all their host, the earth and all that is on it, the seas and all that is in them; and thou preservest all of them; and the host of heaven worships thee. —*Neh. 9:5, 6*

IN SUCH A SKY

There are no words for blueness like today's.
Cerulean, sapphire, turquoise, azure—
Are only words, and this is heaven's pure
Passion of blue; this blue is perfect praise,
So tenderly intense that one who stays
Silent a moment, daring to endure
The soaring glory of it must be sure
It is an act of worship but to gaze.
This hour it has been given us to see,
Unmarred by clouded sight and earthly weather,
The ardent sky the hills of Eden knew.
When man at first was innocent and free
His soul and stars of morning sang together
In such a sky of deeply fervent blue.

Father in heaven, we praise thee for every moment when our hearts are clear and our eyes perceive thy glory in heaven and earth. We praise and glorify thee, O God, in the name of Christ our Savior. Amen.

VII
BLESSED ARE
THE PEACEMAKERS

Blessed are the peacemakers, for they shall be called sons of God.
—*Matt.* 5:9

ANANIAS REMEMBERS

Old Ananias, resting in warm sun,
Spoke softly. "You know well what Paul has done
To win souls to our Lord from pagan ways,
Teaching them righteousness and love and praise."
He paused a little while. His voice was low
When he resumed. "I didn't want to go
And call him brother. I did all I could
To tell myself I had misunderstood
The thing the Master wanted me to do.
To risk my neck and those of others too
By seeking out someone so full of hate
For all of us, seemed mad to contemplate.
But I remembered how the Lord went out
Seeking the worst and neediest ones about—
And who was worse than this fire-breathing Saul?—
And how he bore men's wrath, forgiving all
They did to him. The message came from him.
I could no longer doubt. The way was dim
But I went forth. And when I found Saul, love
And pure compassion filled me from above.
This thought can shake me more than any other—
What if I had not gone and called him brother?"

Lord, help us to be alert and obedient to the promptings of thy Spirit; help us to be thy messengers of reconciliation, peace, and blessing. Amen.

But I say to you that every one who is angry with his brother shall be liable to judgment. . . . So if you are offering your gift at the altar, and there remember that your brother has something against you, leave your gift there before the altar and go; first be reconciled to your brother, and then come and offer your gift.
—*Matt.* 5:22-24

WITH VIOLETS

> Have you seen the far view from a hill
> These beginnings of greenness days?
> Bare trees and earth shimmer
> In a luminous, tremulous haze
> That is not blossom nor leaf
> But blossom and leaf to be,
> A visible aura of hope
> Upon the expectant tree
> And upon the confident earth
> Shining under the promising sky,
> And the air is as tenderly gentle
> And soft as the tentative, shy
> Beginnings of love; and it touches
> With equal persuasive caress
> All in the hill and the valley—
> Oh, there is love to bless
> All the world! And some violets have opened,
> And I picked them for you. I know
> We were angry with one another,
> But the sky and the earth are aglow,
> And anger is all good will.
> I have seen the far view from a hill.

Lord, we thank thee for all that turns our hearts from anger and self-will to peace and good will. Amen.

Remember to extol his work,
of which men have sung.
—*Job* 36:24

RECOMMENDATION

Let there be time enough in every day
For noticing how purely and entirely
Blue the great sky can be, and time to stay
Silent a moment when a star is early
About its shining in a sunset glow,
And time for courteous acknowledgment
When some sky traveler drops a note or two
About the sky's attractions down to you.
Though roofs may be insistent, and the doing
Of necessary things requires intent
And skillful care, occasional sky reviewing
Assists with every down-to-earth event.
However duties crowd, and moments fly,
Let every day have time enough for sky.

Grant us, heavenly Father, to be receptive to the little blessings
that can help to keep our hearts serene. May we not be too
occupied with our work to look up and praise thee for the
splendor of thy work in earth and sky. In all that we do, O
Lord, let thy beauty be upon us, and establish thou the work
of our hands. In Christ's name. Amen.

For we are not contending against flesh and blood, but against the principalities, against the powers, against the world rulers of this present darkness, against the spiritual hosts of wickedness in the heavenly places. Therefore take the whole armor of God, that you may be able to withstand in the evil day, and having done all, to stand. —*Eph. 6:12-13*

THE FAINT HOUR

> So busy in the daytime,
> So weary in the night
> How many hardly notice
> They're wounded in the fight.
>
> But in the earliest dawning
> When light contends with sleep,
> In the unarmored hour,
> How many wake, and weep.

Our Father, we would have thy peace within us and give thy peace to those about us. But we know that if we are to have thy peace we can make no peace with wrong within us and without us. And thou knowest, Lord, that we are often sorely wounded in the struggle. Be with us in the dim hours, Lord, and grant healing for our aching hurts, new strength for the battle, and the peace the world can neither give nor take away. In Christ's name. Amen.

Stand therefore, having girded your loins with truth, and having put on the breastplate of righteousness, and having shod your feet with the equipment of the gospel of peace; above all taking the shield of faith, with which you can quench all the flaming darts of the evil one. And take the helmet of salvation, and the sword of the Spirit, which is the word of God. Pray at all times in the Spirit, with all prayer and supplication. To that end keep alert with all perseverance, making supplication for all the saints. —*Eph. 6:14-18*

HAVING THESE

In any year there will be these:
Comradeship of hills and trees,

Wings and petals, stars and sun,
Victories that must be won,

Words that keep our spirits strong
For the constant war with wrong,

Laughter, grief, and love to share,
Revealing quietudes of prayer,

And little that we need to fear
Having these, in any year.

We thank thee, heavenly Father, for thy abundant provision for our defense against all outward enemies and all inward foes. Grant that we may heartily appropriate and use the good equipment thou hast made available to us. Lord, help us to be joyfully unafraid whatever may befall us, assured that our faith in thee is the victory that overcomes the world. In Christ's name. Amen.

As each has received a gift, employ it for one another, as
good stewards of God's varied grace.   —*I Peter 4:10*

RENEWING FELLOWSHIP

> The dream within the heart,
> The shape within the stone
> Is visualized apart,
> Is realized alone.
>
> No one who would express
> Essentials, can exclude
> The arduous inwardness,
> The searching solitude.
>
> So each creator knows
> The value of each day
> Of fellowship with those
> Who work the lonely way,
>
> And how our minds renew
> Their zest, when we recall
> That every work we do
> Alone, is done for all.

Lord of all truth, we thank thee for the privilege of seeking to
know and to express a portion of the truth. We thank thee for
the sense of fulfillment and peace that comes after hours of
intense concentration on our work. May thy blessing rest upon
all our fellow workers, Lord, and may the hard toil of many
lonely days be lightened by the knowledge that all work done
with the best in us contributes to the good of all. In Christ's
name. Amen.

Lord, thou hast been our dwelling place
in all generations.
Before the mountains were brought forth,
or ever thou hadst formed the earth and the world,
from everlasting to everlasting thou art God.

Ps. 90:1-2

IN ALL GENERATIONS

My father's father died
The year that I was born
And never have I seen his house,
Broad beamed and weather worn,
That sat upon a lonesome ridge
With widely welcoming door.
Its sunny rooms and hallways
Were not mine to explore.

My father's father lived
A life of faithful prayer
And there is gentle fellowship
That we may always share.
Wherever I may go,
Wherever I may be
My father's father's dwelling place
Will always welcome me.

God of our fathers, we thank thee for the fellowship of prayer
that knows no limitations of distance or of time. We pray that as
thy people of all nations lift their hearts in prayer to thee, all
antagonisms and misunderstandings may be blotted out and our
hearts be one with thee and with one another. So may our differ-
ences be transcended and our indifferences be transformed. So
may we work together in earnest good faith for peace among all
nations. Amen.

The Lord bless you and keep you:

The Lord make his face to shine upon you, and be gracious to you:

The Lord lift up his countenance upon you, and give you peace.
—*Num.* 6:24-26

FOR A BUSY FRIEND

Lord of my heart, to my heart's friend
Let all thy gentle peace descend,

Now, in her hours of busy need,
Of weariness of word and deed.

Let thy deep calm encompass all
Her mind and thoughts until the small

Crowding details and quick demands
Are fully met. Lord, guide her hands,

And guard her heart, and grant that she
In all her work, may rest in thee.

Father, we thank thee for our friends, and we pray that we may ever be good friends to them. May we be responsive to their needs, sensing when they are tired and need our silence, when they are sad and need our comfort, when they are sorely tried and need our patience, and when they are glad and need only our companionship in gladness. Most of all, we pray that all our friends may know thy friendship, Lord, and may abide in thee, and thou in them, always. For thy love's sake. Amen.

And thus you shall salute him: "Peace be to you, and peace be to your house, and peace be to all that you have."

—I Sam. 25:6

FOR A NEW HOME

There is a poem in the Book of Books,
A blessing, and a promise, and a prayer
That brings to mind the sound of little brooks,
The scent of lilac on cool sunset air,
The slant of sunlight on a polished floor,
The look and feel of springtime garden loam,
A neighbor's cheerful greeting at the door;
All that our hearts have ever dreamed of home.

"My people," so the promise runs, "shall dwell
In peaceable habitations, and in sure
Dwellings in quiet resting places." Well
And very earnestly we pray, with pure
Devoted grateful friendship, that for you
In your new home, the promise may prove true.

Thou knowest, Lord, the longing in our hearts for secure and peaceful homes for ourselves and for those we love. Yet in our hearts we know, O God, that there can be little security for any of us while any people, near or far, must live in squalor, want, and fear. Our Father, may we be willing to sacrifice and share, to work and pray, so that all people may enjoy the good we seek for ourselves. In the name of Christ. Amen.

Whatever prayer, whatever supplication is made by any man or by all thy people Israel, each knowing his own affliction, and his own sorrow and stretching out his hands toward this house; then hear thou from heaven thy dwelling place, and forgive, and render to each whose heart thou knowest, according to all his ways (for thou, thou only, knowest the hearts of the children of men); that they may fear thee and walk in thy ways all the days that they live in the land which thou gavest to our fathers.　　　　　　　　　　　　　　—II Chron. 6:29-31

FOR PEACE

O God of all the nations, God of all,
Hear thou the prayers all people pray for peace
With dread and horror of what may befall
Unless researches in destruction cease.
Forgive us our mistrust of thee and others,
Forgive our trust in arms that would destroy
Thy image in ourselves and in our brothers,
Annihilating love and faith and joy.

O Father, give us daring hearts, and strict
Self-discipline, and love, securely strong,
Choosing to suffer rather than inflict
On others monstrously disastrous wrong,
Knowing at last that there can never be
Security and peace except in thee.

O God, help us to prove with our lives what we have long professed with our lips, that in thy will for love and reconciliation, and in it alone, is our peace. In Christ's name. Amen.

VIII

BLESSED ARE THOSE
WHO ARE PERSECUTED
FOR RIGHTEOUSNESS' SAKE

Blessed are those who are persecuted for righteousness' sake, for theirs is the kingdom of heaven. Blessed are you when men revile you and persecute you and utter all kinds of evil against you falsely on my account. Rejoice and be glad, for your reward is great in heaven, for so men persecuted the prophets who were before you.
—Matt. 5:10-12

BLESSED ARE YOU

Blessed are you if humbly, without pride
In humbleness, you seek for good to share,
And feel compassionate, unqualified
Deep sorrow for the wrongs men do and bear.
Blessed are you if you are meekly ready
To trust God's righteousness and not your own,
And with a heart of mercy and a steady
Pure faith in good can make peace truly known.

Blessed are you if you so live the best
That you are criticized, condemned, withstood
By those who cannot meet its silent test,
Those who are satisfied with lesser good.
Rejoice in fellowship and good accord
With saints of all the ages, and your Lord.

Father in heaven, grant that if we are persecuted it may truly be for righteousness' and not for self-righteousness' sake. Lord, in all honesty we know that we have seldom indeed been humble, sympathetic, meek, good, merciful, pure, and peaceable enough to embarrass those who are not so. Keep us from assuming that if we are disliked the fault must lie in others and not in us. But if we suffer for earnestly trying to live according to thy will, Lord, may we reverently rejoice to be accounted worthy. In Christ's name. Amen.

For this is thankworthy, if a man for conscience toward God endure grief, suffering wrongfully. For what glory is it, if, when ye be buffeted for your faults, ye shall take it patiently? but if, when ye do well, and suffer for it, ye take it patiently, this is acceptable with God.
—I Pet. 2:19-20 (K.J.V.)

THE UNDERSTANDING ONE

"He who understands will understand"—
Quiet words I hold within my mind
That even in thought I may not reprimand
The trusted ones, intentionally kind,
Who do not understand some words I speak,
Who see no reason in some things I do,
Who are not challenged by the goals I seek
Nor stirred by what I feel is deeply true.

Not always can another's heart respond
With ardor to one's best enthusiasm;
Sometimes we venture, unaware, beyond
Our nearest, and must call across a chasm.
Some do not understand us; but the chill
Is warmed by knowing One who always will.

Help us, Lord, to be understanding even when we are misunderstood. Thou knowest our hearts must always desire the approval of those we love. Grant, Father, that we may love thee and desire thy approval most of all. Grant that all our aims may be so guided by thee that lack of sympathy from others, though it must sadden, cannot discourage us from any good endeavor. And help us wholeheartedly to encourage others as they strive to follow thy will for them, though it may be quite different from thy will for us. In Christ's name. Amen.

For John came neither eating nor drinking, and they say, "He has a demon"; the Son of man came eating and drinking, and they say, "Behold, a glutton and a drunkard, a friend of tax collectors and sinners!"
—*Matt. 11:18-19*

SAYINGS

"They say he let a Negro ride
And even called him 'Sir'!"
"They say she let that colored girl
Sit down and eat with her!"

"They say they're letting city kids
Vacation on their farm."
"They say one of them's been in jail—
They'll do a lot of harm."

"They say he visits old man Jones,
Wild as he is, and queer."
"They say they want a lot of friends—
They won't find many here."

"They say it's getting on their nerves,
The way we stay away."
"Yet they seem happy, with it all—
At least that's what they say."

Grant, Father, that we may be intent to hear the sayings of Christ and do them, not to hear the sayings of gossips and repeat them. May we be ever on guard against the temptation to accept hearsay evidence and to withhold our friendship from others because of idle reports. And help us to maintain our serenity and good humor if we ourselves are talked about unkindly, and our efforts for good misjudged and ridiculed. In Christ's name. Amen.

More than that, we rejoice in our sufferings, knowing that suffering produces endurance, and endurance produces character, and character produces hope, and hope does not disappoint us, because God's love has been poured into our hearts through the Holy Spirit which has been given to us. —*Rom.* 5:3-5

THE WINNER

"I never gave myself crusading airs,"
He said. "I always aimed to be polite.
But liquor stores were offering kids their wares
And all of a sudden I was in a fight.

"I found out things I didn't want to know.
I told a few of them. And then a rush
Of 'phone calls came from people high and low
Suggesting, very nicely, that I hush.

"I didn't hush. I found out more and more.
They started spreading lies about my wife.
Some of our friends quit trading at my store.
I never felt so awful in my life.

"And yet somehow I never felt so good.
I think we'll win—and if we don't, there's zest
In finding I can stand the things I've stood
And not back down. Thank God, I've met the test."

Father in heaven, we thank thee for all those who dare take an unqualified stand for the right, whatever the cost to themselves and those they love. Protect and keep them, Lord, and keep us all from easy compromises. Grant us courage to be true to our most inconvenient convictions and to know the joyous peace of a good conscience. In Christ's name. Amen.

Bless those who persecute you! bless and do not curse them. . . . Repay no one evil for evil, but take thought for what is noble in the sight of all. . . . Do not be overcome by evil, but overcome evil with good. —*Rom. 12:14, 17, 21*

WHITE HOPE

"To hate would not be worthy of us," he said.
A bent dark man, he had been spat upon,
Had acid flung at him from a car that sped
Shrill through the night, and a cross burned on his
  lawn
By men who thought he wasn't good enough
To sit beside them on a public bus.
"Sometimes," he said, "they treat us pretty rough
But we don't fight back, or hate. Hate's not for us."

By overcoming our evil with their good,
Insisting, yet with love, upon their right,
They may help us to do the things we should,
May help us live by our own inner light
Whatever ancient custom may decree.
The colored folk may set the white folk free.

Grant us grace, O Lord and Father of us all, sincerely to repent and utterly to forsake our sins against thy people of other races. Help us to cleanse our hearts of racial arrogance, social pride, and cowardly exclusiveness, and to deal with every person on the basis of character and not of color. Help us, who are so stubborn and so slow of heart, to learn of those we have called inferiors the meaning of Christian love, forbearance, meekness, and self-control. May the long burden of the wrongs we have done them be removed and all thy people worship and live in unity and peace. In Christ's name. Amen.

Enter by the narrow gate; for the gate is wide and the way is easy, that leads to destruction, and those who enter by it are many. For the gate is narrow and the way is hard, that leads to life, and those who find it are few.   —*Matt. 7:13, 14*

HIGH JOURNEY

Up rough roads, in dark weather, we have gone
For long days, and the journey is not done.
The raveling way leads ever up and on
Through forests seldom visited by sun.

Oh, we are weary, weary, and we gaze
With wondering eyes at those who are not tired,
Who walk with laughter level sunlit ways
Bordered by flowers that they have not desired.

But he who calls us to this hazardous
Steep way has faith in our continuing strength,
And we may trust in him who trusts in us
And walks beside us all the road's high length.

Lord, when the way seems very long and very hard and we are worn in spirit, mind, and body, grant that we may not fall or turn aside. Thou who dost not faint or grow weary, renew us moment by moment, that in thy strength we may go on when all our strength is gone. Amen.

Now when John heard in prison about the deeds of the Christ, he sent word by his disciples and said to him, "Are you he who is to come, or shall we look for another?" And Jesus answered them, "Go and tell John what you hear and see: the blind receive their sight and the lame walk, lepers are cleansed and the deaf hear, and the dead are raised up, and the poor have good news preached to them. And blessed is he who takes no offense at me." —Matt. 11:2-6

THE UNOFFENDED

To John, imprisoned for the truth, there came
No word but this, "Go tell him what you hear
And see: the blind receive their sight; the lame
Walk, and the deaf hear words of hope and cheer."
There was no opening of his iron cell,
No sudden restoring of his liberty,
Only the word that others were made well,
Only the news that others were set free.

And, for the blind who never see the light,
For all the deaf who never hear the word,
And all who suffer for the sake of right
With constancy and patience, undeterred
By being misunderstood and set apart,
Christ's blessing on the unoffended heart.

Grant us, O Lord, in all the puzzling days, when nothing goes as we expect it to and there seems no reward for all our efforts and no response to all our urgent prayers—grant us the blessing of the trustful heart. We know that thou art our Savior and Lord and that there is no other, and we thank thee for all thou hast done, and still will do, for others, and for us. Amen.

And one shall say unto him, What are these wounds in thine hands? Then he shall answer, Those with which I was wounded in the house of my friends.　　　　　　　　　—*Zech. 13:6 (K.J.V.)*

BETRAYALS

Before the last betrayal
He often must have turned
Eagerly to Judas
Hoping he had learned
A little understanding;
Hoping he had caught
Something of the spirit
Of all He did and taught.

Before the last betrayal
He often must have met
A glance of cool derision,
A face bewildered, set
In adamant rejection
Of all He tried to share.
Perhaps the last betrayal
Was not the worst to bear.

Thou knowest, O Christ, how often we betray thee by failing to see with thy eyes the possibilities in our problems, by failing to seek thy will in difficult situations, even by willfully turning away from what we know thy will to be. Thou knowest how often we betray thee by our secret discontent and indignation when hard things are allowed to happen to us. Forgive and help us, Lord. Help us to be completely loyal to thee in every thought and word. Amen.

Now before the feast of the Passover, when Jesus knew that his hour had come to depart out of this world to the Father, having loved his own who were in the world, he loved them to the end. —*John 13:1*

HAVING LOVED

How calm the cavern must have seemed,
How restful the stone bed;
Yet soon He left the quiet place
To seek the ones who fled—
To meet with Peter, and console
Him for the words he said.

How good, when it was finished,
Wth nothing more to rend
His heart, to rest! Yet He came forth
To cheer each faithless friend
With eagerness; for, having loved,
He loved—beyond the end.

For all thy love for us we thank thee, Lord. We who are easily offended when others seem to fail us, we who fail every day in loyalty to thee, give thanks to thee for thy unfailing love. We who quickly tire of loving unresponsive people give thanks to thee for thy unwearying love. We who soon come to the end of love and patience give thanks to thee for thy unending love. And we pray, Lord, that thou wilt teach our hearts to love. Amen.

Every one then who hears these words of mine and does them will be like a wise man who built his house upon the rock; and the rain fell, and the floods came, and the winds blew and beat upon that house, but it did not fall, because it had been founded on the rock. —*Matt.* 7:24-25

Blessed is that servant whom his master when he comes will find so doing. —*Matt.* 24:46

WITH US

Too stern for us to build on,
This unconditional stone,
Alluring, terrifying—
If we must build alone.

And following this great pattern
For building strong and true
No unassisted spirit
Can ever hope to do.

But when he sees us striving
To live the truth we hear
Always to us the Master comes,
The Lord himself draws near.

The carpenter of ages
With skillful, patient joy
Works with us on a building
Storms never can destroy.

Father in heaven, we thank thee that the things that are impossible with us are possible with thee, and that thou art with us to the end of the world and beyond. We thank thee, Lord, for all thy blessings to us; unto thee, O God, and to the Lamb be blessing and honor and glory and might for ever and ever. Amen.